THE SECRET LIES OF LIFE

NAVIGATING THROUGH YOUR EMOTIONS TO FULLY HEAL AND FORGIVE

ASHLEY DAVIS

VISION PUBLISHING
HOUSE

Vision Publishing House
support@vision-publishinghouse.com
www.vision-publishinghouse.com

ISBN: 978-1-955297-50-9 (Paperback)
LCCN: 2023916217

To my grandmother, the pillar of strength and wisdom in my life...

When you can't control what's happening, challenge yourself to control the way you respond. That's where your power is.

— SUSAN GALE

CONTENTS

A Letter to My Grandmother

Dear grandmother,

No matter how long it's been since you've been gone, I still cry because I miss you. I missed you when you first left, five years later, and even ten years later I remember the day like it was yesterday, being woken from my sleep, the long drive, and realizing you were gone. It pained me to see you dying, but it would've been even more painful if I wasn't there to see you transition.

After you left, I went into a dark place. My heart was so numb from the grief that was overwhelming, and dealing with everything with granddad, I broke. I was so angry at the world that it turned into hate. I was sad because I missed you, but happy you didn't have to suffer anymore. At sixteen years old, this was a lot to process. I felt so broken as I tried to look for you and

God for guidance. Every moment with you will forever be in my heart.

Thank you, grandma, for being in my life for sixteen years. Thank you for the love you gave me, the hugs you gave me, the food you cooked, and for caring about me. I'm glad that I was by your side when you needed it the most. I thought every month for the first couple of years, why did you have to die? God could've taken granddad, not you. I miss the holidays with you. The holidays without you are so painful. The family tries, but they don't cook like you or give gifts like you. Every holiday felt like a dagger through my heart because it's another year without you. I make jokes because it's easier to smile when I think about you than to cry. I cried for a month straight. Why did you leave? I don't like those people (my family), even though I understand why you left because this family was a mess. We deserve better than your trifling excuse of a husband. I'm sick of everything. Your husband became the wicked person after you died and has the nerve to still want to act like a family. He tries to be like you, but he doesn't love me the way you did because if he did, he would never have put this family through what he did. The way you treated me was real love, and that's how I know granddad's love isn't that real.

I love you, and I will see you soon, angel.

Love Always,
Ashley

X

INTRODUCTION

How did this family get so broken? Let me explain how...

FAMILY ROLL CALL

My grandparents had three kids, and my dad, Cornell, was the oldest. He is the most mature, works hard, and values family. My Aunt Candice is the only girl and the middle child, so she was the favorite of my grandparents. My Uncle Willie is the youngest, and my grandma called him Big Baby. You will definitely find out why that's his nickname.

My dad is married to my mom, Tracy, and they have two kids—my sister Imani and me. Imani and I share an unexplainable bond as sisters and are closer than people think. My Aunt had three kids: Janae, Markail, and Destiny. My Aunt doesn't bring Janae around often, but Markail and Destiny had a typical love-hate relationship. My Uncle Willie was married to Aunt Shaquana with three kids as well: Gabrielle, Hakeem, and Raven. Hakeem was mostly around his mother, so we barely saw him, and Gabrielle and Raven had a typical sisterly relationship. They came through for each other, but they didn't talk as much.

My sister Imani was the first grandchild, which meant she was the favorite grandchild and cousin. Next in line are Janae, Gabrielle, and me. We were all born in the same year, three years after my sister. Gabrielle and Imani share a close bond and are more mature than the rest of us. Then, Markail and Hakeem were born in the same year, which was a year after Janae, Gabrielle, and me. I mostly hung around Markail because we were only six months apart and just bonded. After that, Destiny was born the year after Markail and Hakeem. The youngest, Raven, came a year after Destiny. Destiny and Raven bonded since they are the youngest two grandchildren.

The order in which my grandma loved her grandchildren went as follows: Imani, because she was the oldest and had a bubbly personality; Gabrielle, because she was the smartest in her class, and that made my grandma proud; and then me, as I never gave my grandma a hard time. My grandma loved Janae and Hakeem, but felt indifferent about them. My grandma despised Markail and Destiny. She never really liked them because they were naughty. If Raven weren't her grandchild, she would be happy. Raven had an attitude problem, which I understood because it came from her mother. My grandma only saw a disrespectful little girl, which is why she disliked Raven the most. My grandma had her favorites, but some never knew that she secretly didn't like them. However, I knew exactly why, and I'll further explain that later.

BREAKING BREAD

Thanksgiving this year was at Grandma's house. Grandma's place was the place to be because while the family waited for the food to be cooked, we would either watch a new movie that had just come out or play card games and talk. The adults would typically be in the living room watching a football game, but only if the Cowboys were playing. Imani and Gabriella were close, so they were usually together on the couch in the living room with the adults. Janae and Hakeem rarely came over for the holidays. Raven, Destiny, Markail, and I hung out because we were the ones who loved playing and getting a little loud. This time, I was with them. We were so loud that my grandma said if we didn't calm down, she was going to get a switch from the tree. I said less and moved as far away from them as I possibly could because, baby, I had never gotten a whooping from my grandma, and I wasn't going to say anything.

My grandma prepared ham, spaghetti, chitlins, greens, potato salad, dressing, hot water cornbread, and sweet potato pie. After she finished cooking, all the grandchildren ate in the dining room while the adults dined in the living room. After the meal, we all wrote down our Christmas wishes, although our lists weren't very long as we were getting older, and the adults no longer bought everything on our lists. I decided to put just one thing on my list. Then, my Aunt Candice collected our papers in a bag so the adults could draw names for gift-giving. We then headed to the den to watch a movie together. This time, we watched *Taken 2*, which had come out in October 2012, but my grandma always had access to good movies.

While watching the movie, Markail, Destiny, and Raven sat on the floor, and my grandma asked us about our grades since we had already made our Christmas lists. They didn't say anything, and I mentioned that my grades were alright, but I still had time to improve them. We laughed and changed the topic because of the way my grandma looked at my other cousins with disgust. We definitely needed to change the subject. Eventually, we packed up food because my grandma had cooked so much, and we left. As we left, my grandma came out to wave goodbye to everyone until next month for Christmas Eve.

Christmas Eve was the start of our family's Christmas celebration. We would gather at my grandma's house around 7:00 p.m., open gifts at midnight, and then head home. This time was no different. The adults were in the den setting up gifts, while the kids were in the living room thinking about what gifts we might receive. We all knew because on Thanksgiving, we wrote down our wishes, and the adults would choose a few items from each child's list. The adults exchanged gifts as well. We usually ate first, as my grandma always made sure we had food in our stomachs. She prepared ham, greens, mac and cheese, sweet potato pie, and cornbread.

On this Christmas Eve, I decided to play cards with Markail, Destiny, and Raven so I wouldn't fall asleep before midnight. That plan failed. I ended up falling asleep at the table until 11:55 p.m., when everybody else started cheering to go to the den to open presents. The grandchildren went first. I had asked for a Strawberry Shortcake game for my Nintendo, and my Aunt Shaquana and Uncle Willie got me a couple of Strawberry Shortcake games. My Aunt Candice gave me money. My sister Imani only wanted money, so the aunts and uncles gave her money. Gabrielle, Markail, Destiny, and Raven all wanted clothes, so my parents gave them money to buy what they wanted. My Aunt Candice gave them cute winter shirts, and my Uncle Willie and Aunt Shaquana gave them Jordans or boots along with more winter shirts. The adults exchanged clothes except for my Uncle Willie, who gave my dad the silver watch my dad had wanted.

The highlight of gift-giving came from my grandparents. They watched with joy as everyone opened their gifts, and then it was their turn. My grandma had the grandchildren sit down as she individually gave us our gifts. When it was my turn, she handed me a card with a loving smile, and inside was $50. I hugged my grandma and thanked her.

All the grandchildren were happy, and we all gave our grandparents hugs and expressed our gratitude. The adults brought out a large black garbage bag so the grandchildren could dispose of the Christmas present wrappers. Once we cleaned up my grandma's living room, it was time to go home. We packed up food and presents, and as always, as we got in the car, my grandma was outside waving goodbye to us.

A HEAVY HEART

One of the worst days of my life began on January 18, 2013. It felt like the beginning of the end for my family. My grandma had been the glue that held our family together, and nobody had a clue about what to do or what that would mean for our close-knit family.

On this day, it felt like my whole life started to crumble right before my eyes. My day began just like any other day. I dressed, went to school, attended all my classes, talked with my friends, went to lunch, and left school. It was the spring semester of my first year of high school, and I was looking forward to starting my weekend, or so I thought.

On Fridays, I would usually spend time planning what I wanted to do for the weekend. I often planned to hang out with friends, or my mom would inform me at the last minute about a family event she had planned. But this Friday was different. My mom, Tracy, drove me to my cousin CJ's house to give him some money. My mom always helped her nieces and nephews when they needed it. As we drove to CJ's house, my mom was on the phone talking to my sister Imani, who was in her second semester of college at the time. They discussed how hectic life had become for my sister since she had moved back onto campus.

Suddenly, my mom said, "Oh! While I have both of you here, I have to tell you something." My sister was on the phone, and I was in the car. "Your grandma has cancer."

My heart sank, and I was in shock because I couldn't believe that my grandma had cancer. My eyes filled with tears, and I couldn't help but cry. When my mom shared the news, my whole world seemed to stop. Then, I wondered, "Why did my mom choose this moment, while we were on the way to my cousin's house, to tell me this?"

I realized she could only have been talking about my dad's mom, Lois, because my mom's mom, Julia, had passed away in 2004 due to cancer. In my mind, I thought, "Oh Lord! Not my grandma. Please let her live. She is the only grandma I have left."

My eyes started to well up with tears, and I couldn't help but cry. I cried so hard because cherishing your grandmother is essential, and I had already lost one. I couldn't imagine losing another. My mom told us that my grandmother had known since last November, but she didn't want to ruin the holidays for everyone.

I thought about how life would be after this conversation. I hoped it would bring my grandma and me closer, and I would see her more often. My sister said, "I should have known because she put salt in the potato salad instead of sugar." My grandma's food was always delicious and perfectly seasoned. There was a moment of silence because my sister was the only one who ate the potato salad.

We finally arrived outside CJ's house, and to my surprise, CJ was already outside. CJ came to my side of the car and said, "Hey." My mom and I greeted him while tears still streamed down my face. Thankfully, CJ couldn't see my tears because my coat was so big, covering my eyes. My mom asked how he was and handed him $50. He thanked her and asked how we were doing. My mom responded and said, "Good. What about yourself?"

I still had tears on my face.

He said he was doing well and was glad we were doing good as well. In reality, my whole world had just shattered, and I simply said, "Good."

As the months went by, I wanted to get closer to my grandma while she was still alive, but it wasn't until summertime that I visited her more, which was only once a week.

* * *

Here's some advice:

People receive news differently. When I received my news, I cried and was in shock. Others may try to be strong and not cry. Sometimes, people may tell you news at a bad time, but how you choose to respond is definitely okay. Just remember to stay positive. Everyone thinks of a terminal illness as a death, but staying positive instead of thinking they would die could help with better memories. I had hope that my grandma would beat cancer and that she would just do chemo. So despite how things look, remember to stay hopeful.

FACING THE JOURNEY

In June 2013, when all the grandchildren and parents gathered at my grandma's house, my granddad grilled his famous ribs for his birthday. That was the day I realized how much cancer affected people because we witnessed my grandmother's hair loss. I wanted to cry because I had never seen people lose their hair due to cancer in real life. It felt like my heart was breaking in two. I was confronted with the harsh reality, wishing it was all a dream I could wake up from. I mean, she took that wig clean off. I thought, "Wait, you're not going to give anybody a warning?"

To see her bald traumatized me big time. I mean no hair, just bald. On a more positive note, my grandma was smiling and making jokes while bald-headed. She had come to terms with the hair loss and the toll that cancer would take. Seeing my grandma like that made me think about life and how short it really is. I treated that day like any other day, as I thought I was supposed to. It was indeed a special day.

My grandma was standing at the stove cooking greens and corn-bread to go with our neck bones. After she finished cooking, six out of her eight grandchildren sat outside on a long wooden table with a wooden bench connected, like a vertical picnic table. We talked about everything, from how great the food was to why my cousin Markail had a scar on his stomach. We missed each other and wanted to catch up on life, wanting to know what was new with each other. Afterward, we decided to go to the front yard because the sun was out. It was a beautiful day.

Destiny and Raven played in the green grass in the front yard while the rest of us were on the porch. Imani and Gabrielle then decided to go back inside. Imani and Gabrielle were the oldest, so they were close. They always sat in the den with the adults while Markail, Raven, Destiny, and I were always together. I would typically have to move away from them because they would often misbehave, and we would end up in trouble, which I knew. My grandma would want to discipline us. I sat in the chair on the porch. My Aunt Shaquana and Uncle Willie sat on my right in some more chairs.

I decided to sit on the brick-like seat a few moments later. It was a slick bonus place we sat on in front of the porch. As I returned to my chair, my dad came to join us. He was standing up, leaning against a column as my grandma joked about how my dad looked and that it would be the smallest he would be. I was happy for him because he worked hard to keep his weight down. I thought, "Why wouldn't she encourage him to lose weight?" We all fell quiet because the joke wasn't all that funny, and we just wanted to enjoy the sun while it was still shining outside.

After that, we all went back inside the house to get leftovers to take home. Afterward, everybody got into their vehicles while my grandma waved goodbye on the porch. We all waved back, exchanging our goodbyes and heading for home.

July 7, 2013, was my grandma's birthday. I remember wearing a red dress with a black belt. I wore my favorite-colored dress to see my favorite person, my grandma. No lie, I thought I was so pretty that day that I took many photos. This was the first and only birthday I had with her. My dad and I went to church earlier that day. I normally attended a children's church. Children's church was for younger children starting at age four or five years old until the child turned eighteen. In children's church, we would typically talk about the Word and how it related to younger children. We would also talk about what it meant to believe in God. Children's church was great because I got to see all my church friends. The Word for that day was about waiting on the Lord. It was about waiting on the Lord because he was coming to bless you, but you had to wait. They explained that things never happened overnight. Funny because I remember dreaming that my grandmother survived cancer. I knew it would not be that simple, but I wished it were true. That signified that I needed to slow down and see the situation through. After that message, we played games and/or socialized before our parents came to pick us up.

After my dad picked me up from Children's Church, we went to my grandma's house for a beautiful afternoon filled with tasty food and to visit my grandma. The food she prepared that day was spaghetti, greens, cornbread, and neck bones. Her food was so delicious that we always took leftovers home. Everybody knows when Grandma cooks, she cooks a lot. My grandparents were in the living room watching football, and I watched TV in the kitchen. Even though no one talked, you could feel the love and the bond that everyone shared. It was time for my dad to sleep, so he told me to get ready so that we could go home. I drove home in my dad's truck because at the time, he gave me driving lessons. As I backed out of my grandma's yard, my grandma stood there waving as she always did, and I waved back. This then led me to see her on Sundays. I went to see her every Sunday until November when I got sick and had to take a Sunday or two to get well.

My dad, Cornell, was the biggest reason I went to see my grandma. He was already going weekly, so I asked if I could go with him. That is how I started seeing my grandma more often.

One Sunday in August, I visited my grandma. I came in with my dad. I sat in one of the chairs in the kitchen, and my dad sat in the den talking with my grandparents. To my surprise, my cousin Raven and her mom Shaquana came to my grandma's house. Raven came in with a pouting attitude as her mom threatened to fix her face for her, but Raven still glared. My cousin Raven was the baby of the grandchildren and the one my grandma disliked the most. My grandma was like this with Raven because she would talk back to her parents and had a smart mouth. Honestly, I felt Raven had that attitude because of her mom, so I did not blame her.

My Aunt Shaquana sat down in the chair next to the den. It was at an angle where my grandma could see Raven's face. My Aunt tried to fix Raven's dress, and Raven tried to get away from her mom. My grandma tried to get up to whoop her. I saw her slowly rising out of her chair, trying to solve the problem. I was thinking to myself, "Grandma, go sit down. You have enough to deal with taking all these medications." She had breast cancer, so what was she going to do?

I laughed so hard on the inside because of my grandma's facial expression and the fact that she did not have her teeth in at the time. She tried to mumble words, but could never get it out. After that, I almost turned blue because I was laughing so hard on the inside.

Raven finally let her mom help her with her dress. We all started to eat. This time my grandma made cornbread, of course, with sweet potatoes, greens, and ham. Raven and I ate in the kitchen while everybody else ate in the den. After the adults ate, they watched the rest of the football games. Then, after the football games were over, we all went home.

September 2, 2013, was Labor Day, and my grandma's side of the family had a family reunion at the Mississippi dam. This was the last Labor Day I got to spend with my grandmother. This was also the first Labor Day I got to drive to the dam. Whew, two hours of practice driving! It was hard, but with my dad, he made the experience better since he was the best teacher because of his patience.

We would always go to the Arkabutla Dam in Mississippi as a family reunion tradition for Labor Day. We saw our cousins, uncles, aunts, grandparents, and great-grandparents every year. We talked and played as younger children do. We had a playground and swings we normally played on. The older family members played cards and danced to Southern line dance music.

Before we ate, we always prayed first. I was just living in the moment and was thankful I was with family, but most importantly, I was thankful my grandma was there. This time was different because my grandma called me over to a wooden bench. I typically swung on the swings by the end of a cliff on the dam, so when she called, I hurried up and jumped down to go to her. At the time she was sitting on a bench and eating, and she handed me a Walmart plastic bag. In my mind, I was thinking, "What is this?" Inside the plastic bag was a gold cross-body purse with off-white and gold pearls. At first, all I could do was stare, and suddenly, I heard my grandma say, "If you do not like the purse, you could give it back."

I thought, "Dang! My bad. I've just never seen a purse like this." I thought the bag was unique, so I kept it, and to this day, I still have that purse because anything she gave me, I kept it. I kept it because I knew it was something of hers; for me, it was my way of accepting that she was dying.

After she gave me the purse, I thanked her and returned to the swing. After about an hour, my dad told me he was ready to go, so I drove his truck back home.

* * *

Here's some advice:

Facing your emotions while dealing with someone else can be difficult. During such times, spending time with your loved one becomes important because being there for the people you love means a lot to both you and your loved one.

I wanted to be there for my grandma like she had been all my life, even if my heart broke. You might be scared for your loved one, but trust that they are hiding way more pain, and all you can do is be there and put a smile on their face. Emotions are high because seeing the change is painful for everyone involved. It is okay to cry about the process or even be angry about why God took away your loved one.

THE STRENGTH THAT GIVES

T hanksgiving 2013 would be my last Thanksgiving with my grandma and the family. We gathered as always while my grandma cooked. At first, we were not going to have Thanksgiving this time because my grandma was so ill. She did not want any company, and that was not like her. I was upset and cried because I had already gone a couple of weeks without seeing her because I was sick. In my mind, I thought she did not want to see us, but that was not the case.

After some time, though, my grandma finally said we could come over. I was overjoyed that my Thanksgiving would be complete by being able to spend more time with her. When we arrived, we all wondered where grandma was because she was usually at the door to greet everybody, but this day, my grandad LeRoy told us she was in the bedroom. Everybody else asked where grandma was when they came inside the house as well. I told them that she was not feeling her best and was in bed, so they went to the bedroom to hug and kiss her since we always did that when we first arrived.

All the adults were in the living room, and the grandchildren were in the kitchen, and then my grandma joined us when she finally had the strength to get up. As my grandma cooked, she turned to Destiny,

Raven, and Markail and asked why none of them came to see her except me. On the inside, I wanted to laugh because when she asked, there was nothing but silence, and nobody had an answer. After that silence, we all went into her bedroom to jump on her bed. We jumped so much on her waterbed that it burst. I still wonder how the waterbed burst so easily after all those years of her having it.

After my grandma finished cooking, the grandchildren ate in the dining room so that we were all together since we were so close in age. That was also the Thanksgiving that my Aunt Shaquana saw my cousin Destiny and told her, "Damn, you got big." It made everybody laugh because it was out of nowhere. She was the Aunt who always acted like she was small. My sister brought her boyfriend at the time, and my cousin Markail was so overprotective that he stared at the guy all night as he was eating. Markail was staring at him while he ate because that's what "little big" guy cousins did to ensure their girl cousins were protected. He told the guy that if he broke my sister's heart, he would give him Benadryl as he raised his left arm and Nyquil as he raised his right arm. It was hilarious. We all laughed but knew how serious he was.

At one point, we got on the piano my grandma had sitting in her dining room, and my younger cousin Destiny was pressing on a few keys as they often did because they did not know how to play. I knew a little because of my previous piano lessons, so I played a song from middle school that I had just graduated from that past spring. My grandma asked me to play some music. I tried, but I forgot the notes.

As the night continued, the grandchildren and parents came to the den. We enjoyed each other so much that we all laughed. Soon everyone was fully packed, ready to call it a night. Everyone was winding down. We all packed plates full of Thanksgiving food and went home. I was glad I had a chance to go over there because I knew I would miss her, and all the time spent with my family meant every-thing to me.

* * *

Here's some advice:

It's always good to let out pain and emotions because every-thing is sensitive at this point. Not knowing if your loved one would be okay is scary. Feeling sad, happy, or heartbroken is normal because these stages that your loved one goes through are hard. It's hard on everyone, and what better way to ease your emotions than being with family who feel the same? Having hope also helps because no one wants to think about their loved ones not getting better and dying.

THE PREPARATION

After Thanksgiving, on December 15, my mom told me my grandma Lois was in the hospital. At the time, I attended Central High School, and across the street was a Methodist hospital where she was a patient. Since it was across the street, all I had to do was walk. I walked across the street with my mom's information about what wing my grandma was on; of course, it was in the cancer unit.

When I walked into my grandma's room, it was dark and gloomy. The only light was the TV in the room. My grandma and her children were in the room.

I hugged my grandma. I was mostly hugging her enlarged boob since she had breast cancer. I thought, "Dang, she is not going to move her watermelon boob so I can hug her." I asked about a chair because there was only a couch that seated three, which was already at capacity. So my Aunt Candice and I got a chair from an empty room nearby. We laughed about how I had just stolen a chair and the fact that I got away with it without anybody seeing us. I pulled my chair next to my grandma. I asked how everybody's day was, and everybody said good, which changed the room's mood.

After a while, my mom arrived shortly after her shift, which was convenient since she worked at the same hospital. Things took a turn when my grandma started to talk about her funeral arrangements. I tried hard to put on a brave face and make light of the situation. The nurse came to discuss her plans for going home or to hospice. At first, my grandma decided that she wanted to go back home. Everybody in the room looked at my grandma as if saying, 'You cannot be serious about that decision.' The only reason we looked at her like that was because, at the time, she and my granddad LeRoy were moving to another house. Besides, her house had a lot of dust in it. I thought, "Why kill yourself sooner that way?" It might have been selfish to want her to just be comfortable, but I just wanted my grandma to live longer.

She then changed her mind and said she would go to the hospice. She told my dad, uncle, and auntie where she wanted to be buried, which was by my great-grandma, who died in 2009. My grandma continued sharing the details of how she wanted her funeral program to go. She told us who she wanted to speak at her funeral service. She further explained to us what songs she wanted to be played, and one of them was "Amazing Grace." Then, she told everybody in the room not to cry at the funeral.

I gave her a look that said, "Yes, okay, like be real, grandma."

My grandma said that she wanted my mom's sister, Pam, to sing another song, but she declined to sing because she would be in the pulpit crying way too much.

After that extremely tough conversation, we all went home afterward. Yes, I cried myself to sleep that night because my grandma realized her time was running out. I was not ready to talk about her leaving. It was hard seeing the stages she went through, but hearing her plan for the funeral was too much to handle for me.

* * *

Here's some advice:

Seeing your loved ones in the hospital and trying not to cry is one of the hardest things to do. However, instead, try to turn it into something positive with a joke or a simple smile. Having that difficult conversation about end-of-life plans is necessary so your loved one can have a plan for their funeral. Many people find peace in knowing their time is coming to an end, and they want to make everything right for when they transition. After those conversations, it's okay to feel sad and hurt because honestly, no one is ever really ready for "the talk."

THE "HOSPITALITY" GUEST

The following week, we went to visit my grandma in the hospital. My sister and I went in and hugged her like everybody else who entered her room. In the room were me, my sister, my cousin Destiny, my cousin Raven, and other family members visiting my grandma. Everybody had an enjoyable time as we talked and laughed. Then suddenly, a lady I had never seen before entered. When she entered the room, you could sense something was off as she gave off this negative energy. I just wanted to know who she was.

When she walked in, she immediately sat down, which was unusual since everyone else who came in hugged my grandma first. She began talking to my grandma about how she felt my grandma had given up on her fight against breast cancer, all the while my grandma sat there on her deathbed. The lady lectured my grandma, suggesting that attending church more might have changed her fate. My grandma explained that she hadn't returned to church because there were only ten members left, and she had taken time off from attending due to her mother's death. It was frustrating to see my grandma, while facing a terminal illness, having to justify her choices to someone who clearly didn't care.

Before the lady left, she concluded her visit with a prayer. However, her choice of scripture was unsettling. She prayed about a passage from the Bible that spoke of a person turning into salt when they looked back.

> *Then the LORD rained upon Sodom and upon Gomorrah brimstone and fire from the LORD out of heaven; and he overthrew those cities, and all the plain, and all the inhabitants of the cities, and that which grew upon the ground. But his wife looked back from behind him, and she became a pillar of salt.*
>
> — GENESIS 19:24:26

I thought, "What does this have to do with my grandma?" I opened my eyes and started to look around to see if anybody else felt the same way about this "prayer."

The prayer ended, and I was confused. She tried to leave, but my family insisted she hug my grandma. The lady turned around and hugged my grandma, but my grandma turned her head, knowing she did not want to embrace the lady, and the lady left. We all stared at one another, wondering what that was about. We talked until some family members left, and then we knew it was time to go.

The following week, we went to the hospice where my grandma had chosen to go. I had never heard of hospice before, so I initially thought it was a place meant to help my grandma recover, but it was the opposite. It was to help her "be comfortable" until she passed. This time, my Auntie Shannon was there. It had been years since I had seen her. I rarely saw her because she lived in Chicago.

When I came in, I hugged my grandma, and this time, she offered me a chocolate chip cookie. I was happy to take the cookie. I also hugged my Aunt Shannon and said hey.

When I sat down on the couch, my Aunt Shannon and my grandma were talking about how they were little and always played with each other and how close they were. My grandma said she used to play dress up with Aunt Shannon and how much fun they used to have. I sat there as I watched and listened to my grandma and her sister as my Aunt tried to get my grandma to eat a sandwich. My Aunt continued to say, "Here, eat this" as she shoved the sandwich to my grandma's lips, airplane style.

Suddenly, I heard, "I don't want that shit" coming from my grandma. My grandma turned to me and said, "Oh, excuse me, baby."

I wanted to laugh, but I had seen how mad my grandma was and how heartbroken my auntie was when my grandma said that. So the room fell silent, and after an hour, I called my mom, and she came to pick me up because my Aunt had gone home by that time, and my grandma had fallen asleep.

My cousin Janae was adopted by my Aunt Candice, whom I did not know until my mom told me later in high school. My mom explained that her adoptive parents did not agree, so the adoptive dad often kept Janae, and we rarely saw her. That explained a lot because growing up, we saw Janae a lot, and when we were older, we did not see her as much. It made me wonder where she was most of the time. I wanted her to experience moments with the rest of the grandchildren, but it did not work out that way.

My grandma begged to see Janae just one last time before she died, and Janae had a chance to visit my grandma before she was heavily medicated, as my mom said. No matter if she was adopted. I thought of her as my cousin and never saw or treated her differently.

* * *

Here's some advice:

If you feel negative energy from someone, believe that. The way that people will try to kick you while you're down is very low and unacceptable. However, continue to show up for your loved ones despite how others may act. Showing up is a simple way to show your loved ones you care. Hugs and kisses to and from a loved one heal a lot. Going will also help you as well. It might be hard to be strong, but in the end, it will be worth it. Let it out in a safe space because it won't get easier.

NAVIGATING THROUGH THE ACCEPTANCE

Christmas Day 2013 was the last Christmas we spent with my grandma. At this point, she was still in hospice, and the nurse there gave her medicine to ease her pain. My grandma only woke up for a couple of seconds in the morning and then slept again. My grandma slept all day, but we still went to see her. When we would go, we would kiss her cheeks and hug her so she could feel us there.

For Christmas, the grandchildren all sat around her bed. We talked, and of course, some of my cousins, Raven, Destiny, Markail, and my sister Imani, tried to wake my grandma up by poking her. I said, "If she wakes up, I am going to tell her who it is" because I knew that if she woke up, she would wake up swinging. I did not want to get hit.

We went to take photos around the hospice facility because the place looked beautiful. The hospice facility had many places to take pictures. The Christmas tree, the grand piano, the outside, and the fireplace were great spots. We enjoyed that day with family despite my grandma not being awake. We made it the best Christmas with all things considered.

On the next visit to the hospital, on December 28, the lady with the negative energy, whose name I still did not know, was back with a choir from the ten-member church. I tried to figure out why they were there because the last time she spoke with my grandma, she made it seem like she had given up. The choir came and sang. They sang this beautiful song about a home in heaven for my grandma. Afterward, everybody in the room got up and prayed when the choir was done. The choir called my grandma home in the prayer, which was why I broke the prayer. This was the only time I was heartbroken and mad in prayer because the choir knew my grandma would pass soon, but I did not want it to be true. To break prayer meant I had to let go of the two people's hands and open my eyes in the worship, which is a big no-no for worshippers. I could not imagine losing my grandma so soon.

After that prayer, I went to the bathroom in my grandma's room with my sister and cried my eyes out, sitting on the toilet. When I got up, my sister hugged me and stood with me until I was ready to return to the room. I never really cried in public. I always cried when people were not around, unless it was somebody close to me, like my mom or sister.

We all got in the car, and my mom and sister had a conversation about how my grandma would pass away in January. My heart broke because January was only a couple of days away. My birthday was on December 30. So, for my birthday, I decided not to go to the hospice because I wanted to have a happy birthday, but I promised that I would go the next day.

On December 31, I went to the hospice to see my grandma. I always went to visit, and this time, I wanted to make up for not going the day before. I just sat there with her. She still was under the medication that only had her wake up a little a day, and I watched whatever was on the TV in her room. I called a guy I had been seeing because I was upset he didn't come to my birthday party because it was his and his girlfriend's anniversary—like I cared. I thought, "*I hope my grandma doesn't hear me*," but I continued to go off on him, and all he could do was apologize.

I got off the phone after ten minutes and sat with my grandma in silence, but I still appreciated being there with her. After about two hours, my mom came to pick me up and took me home.

Memories with Grandma

- My grandma always used to say I got my hair from her. She would be like, "You know, I'm part Cherokee." I didn't doubt that my grandma had nice hair because my mom's hair was not like mine. I did doubt she was Cherokee though because she just looked straight-up black. I always laughed, though. How could I tell when she had a slicked-down ponytail all the time?

- When I was six, my mom's mom passed, and all I could remember was sitting down at the funeral, and all of a sudden, we had to get up. I walked behind my sister as we walked behind the casket, and when I looked up, I saw my other grandma, my dad's mom. I couldn't help but to be surprised because I wasn't expecting her to be at my other grandma's funeral.

- When I was in the third grade, I had to go to the hospital because my breathing wasn't doing well, and I passed out. I had to stay for four days and three nights at the hospital. One of those days, my grandma came, and they were about to take me to another room. My grandma went with me as they rolled me into another room, holding my hand, and all I could do was smile because my grandma was there for me, which was why I always stayed by her side when she was sick.

- One day when I was in elementary school, my grandma had to take my sister and me for the day since my parents had to work. I was minding my own business in her house when my grandma yelled at me, saying, "That's why you are sick now because you don't have on socks!" Afterward, I rolled my eyes because what did my socks have to do with being sick? When I was finished, she yelled again that she was going to Piggly Wiggly and that I needed to hurry up.

- One day, I was over at my grandma's house. I asked her to help me with my math homework. Baby, when I got my paper back, I got an F. I should've done the homework on my own; at least I would've failed, not both me and my grandma.

- My grandma got me hooked on different foods since I was always over there because my mom worked until eleven, and my dad was at work. So, my grandma would pick us up from school. My grandma had me hooked on apples with salt. Sounds crazy, I know, but it was so good. In the morning, we would eat red smoked sausage sandwiches with mayo and brown smoked sausage sandwiches with grape jelly. Honestly, whatever she made, I always ate it.

- I was out with my grandparents one day, and Granddad was driving. My grandma was yelling at Granddad so much because he was going in the wrong direction. They were trying to drop me off at the beauty shop, but my granddad kept missing the exits, so all I heard was "LeRoy...LeRoy... LeRoy." I felt so bad for Granddad that day. I know he wanted to jump out of the car, and I didn't blame him.

- One day, my grandma commented on my Facebook photo:

"grandma loves u being Ashley Alise Davis too.
Love seeing all of your pictures. Everything
always looks so good together. U have very
good taste. U also dress like I would or did
back in the day. Have a good weekend. Love
grandma."

I replied:

"Thank you grandma, I hope to see you soon."

- When I was in the fifth grade, my grandma had my sister
  and me because my parents went out of town for the
  inauguration in Washington, DC. Of course, while my
  grandma was there, it was probably 4:00 a.m., and there was
  yelling. She was yelling that we needed to hurry up because
  she was going to be late.

- One day, we all got in the car with our red smoked sausage
  sandwiches, and she took me to my elementary school. Tell
  me why we were so early? We arrived before the before-
  care workers, who came in at 5:00 a.m. She started yelling,
  asking where the workers were so she could go to work.

- One day, with the straightest face, I kept telling my
  grandma, "They're not here because it's not time yet." So,
  she asked why they didn't open early, as if Before Care
  wasn't early enough. When a worker finally arrived, I was
  so glad to go in because it was too early for all that. To make
  matters worse, my sister dropped in after me around 5:15
  a.m., and she was in high school, which didn't start till
  7:15 a.m.

- When I was in middle school, my sister always picked me
  up since she had her truck, but this time was different. I was

waiting for what felt like an hour after school in the heat, but I couldn't call my sister because I couldn't bring my phone to school. I decided to head back up to the school to find my sister, and when I finally went up there, my sister still hadn't arrived.

• All of a sudden, I heard someone yelling at me, and of course, it was my grandma. She yelled, asking me if I saw her truck. I thought, "Baby, I'm not looking for your truck. I'm looking for my sister." I finally got in, and my sister was in the truck. My sister apologized, saying her truck had broken down, and then she called Grandma. I was just glad I got to go home.

Grandma and I have shared some good times together. I am happy that I still have these memories as a source of comfort and inspiration whenever I desire to take a journey back in time.

* * *

Here's some advice:

Christmas is always an important time to spend with family because family is all you have. Make the best out of situations because you would rather remember happy moments than sad moments. To see your loved one sedated is hard and can definitely be overwhelming, but I learned that it was better because your loved one doesn't feel the pain. Still, being by their side might be hard, but they still know you showed up, and it's better to be there with them instead of just thinking about them.

NEW YEAR IN DISBELIEF

On January 1, 2014, I didn't get to sleep until 3:00 a.m. and woke up at 6:00 a.m. to use the bathroom. As I was walking across the hall to my upstairs bathroom, I saw my mom at the bottom of the stairs, saying good morning and asking if I would like to go to the first-of-the-year sale at Dillard's with her. With crust in my eye, I simply looked at her, said, "No, ma'am," turned the other way, and went back to sleep after my mom left.

Suddenly, my sister shook me and told me that Grandma had passed. I was jolted awake from my sleep and instantly wide awake. My body was in shock, and it felt like a terrible nightmare that was all too real. My sister was in a panic, urging me to hurry up and get dressed. I looked at my sister and asked who would tell Dad since he was sleeping. I planned to talk to my mom, and Imani would wake my dad up to inform him that his mom had passed. I said no, but my sister went ahead and woke him up to share the news.

I looked at my phone and noticed I had several missed calls. I called my mom back, and she went off on me when she answered. She asked, "You were just up. What happened? Why didn't you answer my call?" I told my mom I was sorry and that I had gone back to sleep, and my sister and I were on the way to the hospice.

That was the most silent car ride of my life. I did not talk because I had nothing to say. My sister blasted gospel music, which made me want to cry even more. The alternative would have been that I went with Mom, and not go to the first-of-the-year sale at Dillard's because the sale started at 8:00 AM, and we would've been early. Or instead, me and my mom would've visited my grandma at the hospice facility. However, if we had been there, my grandma would've opened her eyes and taken her last breath. I thought about how it would have messed my soul up to see my grandma take her last breath. *Lord, bless the people who have seen somebody take their last breath. I couldn't even bear the pain.*

"We finally arrived at the hospice facility. We had to sign in as always, but the lady knew who we were and why we were there, so she let us know that we could go right in this time. That was the first time I shed tears in public. We went into my grandma's room. When we went in, it was dark and gloomy. I sat on the couch where I always sat and stared at the lifeless body of my grandma. I was in shock, so it was easier to see her lifeless body like any other time after she could not speak. I remained silent until Auntie Shaquana came in with a loud cry. She cried so hard and said, "I am sorry… I am sorry… I am so sorry."

I broke down and cried because that was the type of cry that always made me cry. I went outside the room to take a break. Imani told me we had to get my cousins Destiny and Markail since they were at home, and my Aunt Candice was in the room grieving. It was not far. When we were in the car, I asked why they were not with their mom. Imani turned to me and said, "Not today." I replied, "Okay, I just asked."

We finally picked them up and silently went back to the hospice. I went to my two cousins, Raven and Destiny, to talk to them, and Destiny said she wished Grandma would have made it to 2014. I said, "Well, at least she did make it to 2014."

It went quiet. Then suddenly, I saw my grandma get carried out on a stretcher with a white sheet covering her whole body. It tore me up on the inside because I realized she was gone. Since she was taken out of the room, they told the family we had to clean the room, as if my grandma dying four hours ago was not enough. I stood with my sister, while I tried not to cry. Then, my cousin Markail, who was standing behind us, hugged us from the back, resting his arms on our shoulders, and he lowered his head. To me, that meant we are in this together, as we cleaned her room out. After we cleaned the room, I thought the day was over, but it was far from over. We went back to my grandma's house right after she died.

All the grandchildren were sitting on the floor in the den, and Auntie Shaquana told the other adults that the children needed to eat since nobody had eaten that day. They ordered Church's Chicken, and the kids ate in the other den as we watched Chucky since nobody wanted to talk. The adults had to gather in the kitchen to arrange the obituary— my grandma's full name, her children's names, her grandchildren's names, and the plans my grandma had when she was at the hospital. Next, it was time to pick out an outfit. They picked a lovely lavender suit, her favorite color, and all the jewelry she loved to wear. When everything was finished, we all went home.

It was now January 3. A few days had passed since my grandma died, and my mind was everywhere. I went back to school— thank God— because I wanted to get my mind off the grief and try to be "happy" again. It was also a couple of days before my mom's upcoming missions trip, so we all went to Cheddar's to eat dinner. At dinner, my mom told us that my Aunt Shaquana and Aunt Candice argued over something small and dumb. Families fight over the dumbest things, when in reality, we need to agree and be around each other. My mom told us she did not have time for that because Grandma had just died, and she was about to leave for a missions trip to the Dominican Republic.

On January 5, my mom had a once-in-a-lifetime chance to go to the Dominican Republic to be a missionary nurse. For months, she debated on whether she should go on the trip or not because my grandma was dying. My sister and I tried to tell my mom that she should go because we did not know when my mom would get another opportunity. My mom finally decided to go on the trip weeks before my grandma died because my grandma told her she should go. After my grandma died though, my mom worried she would not make it to my grandma's funeral. She tried to explain the situation to my granddad LeRoy, but my granddad told her no, he would not change the date. My mom had already booked the flight, so she could not cancel, which meant missing the funeral.

January 10 was the day of my grandma's wake. I went to school, but knew I had to leave early. I thought about everything that would transpire after leaving school, and I became anxious waiting for my sister. I kept going to the office to see if she had been there to pick me up. The person at the office's front desk asked who would be checking me out. She asked if it would be my grandmother. I froze and thought, "No, but that is who I would see in a casket." I explained that my sister would check me out, and the lady told me she would call my class once my sister arrived to get me. My sister took too long for me, so I kept calling her because I did not want to be at school and wanted to see my grandma. My sister kept telling me she was close to my school, but she was not close enough in my mind. Finally, my sister called and said she had made it. I went downstairs to the office and asked her why it took her longer than expected to get me. She did not reply. She said nothing once she came to pick me up. I was excited to leave school, but had no idea how to feel about the wake.

We drove to the funeral home, and suddenly, my mood changed. It was a dark presence that came over me. I shut down and did not talk, which was never like me, especially around my sister. I was so numb; I didn't know if I was happy, sad, or mad. I realized, then, that this would be one of my first goodbyes as we went in. We had to search around because many families were there with their deceased family members. We finally found the room where they displayed my grandma for us to view. I saw her body and had to tell myself she was asleep to ease my pain. The pain of seeing my grandma in the casket was so overwhelming, that my emotions froze to protect me from the pain.

I still could not believe that my grandma was gone. I could not think that my only living grandmother had passed. I sat in this black chair in front of her casket, too numb to cry or react. The only thing that got me through was my sister being there. A lady in a green chair beside me told me, "Sorry for your loss." I never understood why people say sorry for your loss. It irritated my soul when people said that.

I turned around and saw my cousin Hakeem and wondered why he was crying so hard. He cried like how I cried when I found out she had died and saw her body lifeless. I then realized he was not there the day she died, so this was the first time he saw her body. All the other grandchildren, except one, were there the day she passed. I went to comfort him without hesitation because that was just what our family did. After I went to comfort Hakeem, I ran into my Uncle Willie. I accidentally asked my uncle if he was okay. I knew it was a terrible question because you could see that he was not okay. His mom had just died. He replied, "Yes," but I saw the pain in his eyes, which said otherwise.

After about two hours, we finally went home. When we got off the funeral home parking lot, I became myself again and told my sister I never wanted to go to another wake. She asked, "Why not?" I replied, "I hate to see dead bodies." However, I still would have gone for my grandma's even after knowing what a wake was.

January 11, the morning of the funeral, was dreadful. That morning felt like time stood still. I tried to make sure I looked my best in an all-black dress that I loved to wear with my black wedge heels and black and gold sunglasses to cover my tears. I had my hair in a body wrap style to match the occasion. I rode in the car with my sister because my mom went out of town, and my dad rode in the limo with all my grandma's children.

The ride to the funeral home was quiet. We knew what was about to happen, but remained in good spirits. All we did was listen to music in the car, but no matter how loud the music was, my thoughts drowned everything out. All I could ponder about was how I had to see my grandma's body and how it would be the last time. We finally made it to the funeral home, and to my surprise, my Aunt Pamela and cousin Leana were there because they also knew and loved my grandma. This was the same Aunt my grandma wanted to sing at her funeral, but could not, which was understandable. My Aunt and cousin were from my mom's side of the family, so to see my mom's side support my dad's side made me tear up, but it was short-lived.

We had to hurry up and get back in the car to prepare for the funeral lineup. The procession was one of the longest parts of the day. It was the lengthiest hour-and-a-half drive to the church. The car was filled with nothing but music to uplift our spirit, but it still did not help me. We finally arrived at the church, and the ground was covered with rocks. I was trying to keep my balance because I had on wedges. We lined up in front of the church, waiting for the funeral car to arrive.

I stood next to Hakeem, and we joked about my other cousin Daisy because she wore a short dress in January. We did not like her anyway because of her attitude. As soon as the church door opened, you could see that it was filled with many people. We walked in one by one, and I was in front of my uncle, and behind me was his son, Hakeem. As we walked down what seemed like a long church aisle, I tried not to look at either side of me because my mood changed to numbness. I did not speak or try to look at anyone because I was focused only on the funeral. I noticed everybody in front of me had kissed my grandma on the cheek, and when I went up to the coffin, I kissed her for the final time. It was such a cold kiss, not like the warm kisses I used to give her cheeks. I was nervous because I thought she would rise from the casket. To see her body meant her death was real, and I wanted her to rise from the dead, but not actually.

As we took our seats, I sat there frozen. I did not remember the funeral, because in my head, I pondered about the last time we saw and thought about never being able to see my grandma again.

I got this feeling in my gut that I did not want to be on earth, but not in a suicidal way. I wanted an encounter to visit heaven to talk to her about everything that was going on and then come back to earth. I tried to deal with grief, but I was so hurt that I did not know how to express it without crying. I tried to cry during the funeral, but only a tear came out. I remember seeing that nasty spirit lady once again and her choir on the program, as they sang by my grandma's casket. I thought that was interesting. After all, she tried to shame my grandma because she "gave up" on her battle with breast cancer, as she implied and stated.

Then, the pastor of the church gave us the word of the day. The message was about how the dead move on and how they are in a home up above and told us my grandma was in a better place. He talked about how God called her home and how great of a woman my grandma was. Next, were words of expressions from my aunts and cousins from my grandma's side of the family. Following that was the song "Amazing Grace." I could not even get to the word *grace*, and I cried. After that, were words of comfort. Honestly, a comforting comment was needed since it was a long day, and it was the only thing I needed besides a hug. A quiet reading of the obituary was next.

I did not want to read the obituary because I had already scanned through it before the funeral started. Instead, I daydreamed through the acknowledgments and another song. I stopped listening and was just in denial about the funeral. The last thing on the obituary was a eulogy and a tribute. The pastor returned to give final words about how we should proceed to the burial, and everyone who was not going to the burial could go to the repast. The casket went down the aisle, and we followed.

I got back in the car with my sister, and we looked at each other and cried nonstop. She covered me with her arms as we continued to cry together. We stayed like that until we heard cars crank up as a signal to head to the burial. It was a five-minute drive, which was not bad. We made it to the burial, and as we walked toward the casket, my Aunt (my grandma's sister) was talking to my granddad. Both were crying and saying that my grandparents had been married for forty-five years and how heartbroken he must have been.

Looking back, it broke my heart to see him like that, as I cried. I wish I had saved those tears because my grandad was never worth one of my tears.

This was the slowest walk of the day. I walked side by side with my sister to the burial. As I walked toward the grave, I saw my mom's sister, who always told funny jokes. At the time, I was not in the mood and hoped she would not say anything to me to make me lose focus on what that day represented. Still, I could only focus on the day's sadness and seriousness. We were given roses, and we placed our roses on the casket, and I stood farther back with my sister. My cousin Markail came between us and held our hands, and you could tell Destiny and Raven were jealous. They made a scene about Markail not holding their hands. I held Destiny's hand while Imani held Raven's hand so that we could be in unity. That moment was precious because it was the grandchildren together trying to help comfort each other through a sorrowful day.

The burial was finally over, and it was time for the repast. The repast was held in a small church-like building. It had an upper area stage, and the lower level had a wooden floor. The grandchildren were seated on the stage. It felt as if it was on a pedestal. The church fed us and gave everybody sodas. We were all full except Markail, who asked for another slice of chocolate cake, which was my favorite. After he ate that slice, he asked the lady if he would like another slice of chocolate cake. The lady looked at him dead in the eyes and asked whether she was supposed to be Aunt Jemima, with such a nasty attitude. After her bipolar moment, we all looked shocked because she had asked if we wanted anything. We were confused when she made that statement. We all talked about her saying that to us as we sat there.

Later that night, I changed clothes for my friend's birthday party. I went to Buffalo Wild Wings with friends I had known since ninth grade to take my mind off the funeral from earlier that day. That night was just what I needed to get my mind off how I was feeling.

* * *

Here's some advice:

Entering into the dark side of grief can be normal. I never knew it existed, but the overwhelming amount of sadness and heartbreak is real. My advice in this state is to let it out. Any emotion you have, express it, whether it's by yourself or with your support system. A support system is so helpful in times when you think you can't go on with life. Feeling numb, heartbroken, mad, relieved, and sad is normal for grief; never let anyone tell you differently. Grief can take over, but never ever sit at home after a terrible event. Go out and take your mind a little bit off grief.

THE SECRETS UNRAVEL

On January 17, 2014, I went to the beauty shop to get my hair done, and after three hours, my sister came and picked me up since she was still in town. As I gathered my things, I overheard what my sister and the beautician talked about. My sister told our beautician that my granddad had already moved on and had a girlfriend. My beautician was a family friend of my mom, so she knew both sides of my family. They talked for another ten minutes because my beautician could not believe the news.

After the conversation, we headed to the car. Once we were in the car, I asked my sister who the new girlfriend was, but my sister never answered. I realized she was not telling me, so I dropped the topic. I wondered who this new person was whom my grandad had moved on with so fast. As we were going home, we talked about other things, but never addressed the question I asked previously. Months went by before I received an answer.

The rest of January was filled with tears and heartbreak. I pretty much cried the entire month. Stage one of grief was the hardest stage to go through, which was denial. I knew my grandma had died because I saw her, but on the inside, I couldn't accept that she was gone. One day my grandma was here, and now she wasn't. I thought it was a dream and how any day, I knew I would go see my grandma soon. My heart was throbbing every day I woke up and had to realize she was gone.

Why does my heart hurt so much? I miss talking and seeing her. *What do I do now?* I pray to God every day, asking how to live life without her. I had to delete her number, so I couldn't try to call her. I looked back on Facebook to read her beautiful words, but all I could do was cry. I was trying to move forward by taking pictures, but the truth was I was hurt by all this heartbreak and did not know what to do about it.

I felt so guilty because I wanted her to see what I looked like for my birthday party five days before she passed. My mind was everywhere, but nowhere at the moment. I wanted my grandma back so bad. *Why did you have to leave so soon? What am I supposed to do now?* All I can do is cry and cry.

One month since my grandma passed, and I couldn't even start to grieve. My head was in a daze, and denial was killing me. I was still in the denial stage because it didn't make sense to lose both of my grandmas almost ten years apart. I saw her the day before, wishing I could hold on to that day, over and over. When I finally tried to get myself together by the end of February, I began to reflect on everything that had happened so far, and all I could do was cry and scream. I transitioned from denial to slowly accepting my grandmother's death. I honestly don't remember much about what happened during that month of February, except that I took a lot of pictures and survived everything somehow. My world was turning dark, and my soul was so heartbroken.

March finally arrived. During this time, I began to experience grief even more. Every year for my mom's birthday, since I was young, her dad and brother would come visit. My mom would always pick up my granddad and uncle from the airport and bring them to the house. As my mom was driving, she and Granddad were talking, and I mostly tuned them out until my granddad Darnel (my mom's dad) mentioned my grandmother's name, and it caused me to break down on the inside. I hadn't heard her name in a couple of months, so it triggered my tears all over again. This was such a difficult, emotional time for me.

When we arrived home, I cried in my room, and stage two began with sadness. I realized she wasn't here on earth, but in my heart, she was going to always be there.

On May 26, 2014, my granddad LeRoy invited us over for Memorial Day, which sounded great because I missed him, and the food was good. My sister was home from college, so we both went to my granddad's house, which was an hour's drive away. It was not too bad of a drive. We pulled up, and he came to open the door. We hugged him and walked in to sit at the kitchen bar.

To my surprise, the rude lady who visited my grandmother in the hospital was there, so my brain became confused. As I looked confused, I turned to my sister and thought, "Was this the person she and my beautician were discussing?" I texted my sister secretly, asking if this was the woman. She replied, "Yes," and that was all I needed to know. It was the same evil-spirited lady from the hospital and the funeral.

I asked my granddad where the bathroom was, and the lady answered instead and said it was down the hall. I thought, *I did not ask you*, so I asked him again where the bathroom was. He answered, "Down the hall."

I replied, "Thanks!" I went to the bathroom. I was so furious that he moved on, and not only that, but with her. I said, "f——k this m ——r s——t b——h f——k b——h a——s s——t" all within a minute under my breath. I collected myself, used the bathroom, and returned to where everyone was sitting again. My granddad was finally finished with the food, so we made plates and sat back down to eat. We all dined together, and I thought about going home. We eventually left, and I was thankful because I was so hurt and mad. All I wanted to do was go home and cry.

That situation broke my heart. *How could he have another girlfriend so soon?* My grandma, *his wife*, just died, and it seemed like my granddad couldn't care less. I honestly didn't know how to express or even start to explain my feelings. I honestly lost it. I was seeking love in all the wrong places, telling multiple guys I liked I was suicidal, which was crazy because I wanted to visit, not stay. I started listening to "What Now" by Rihanna. It was therapeutic, especially because of what was about to happen next with my granddad which caused me grief. One line in the song was "I just can't figure it out," and that was true. I felt so lost and confused that I didn't know how to figure my feelings out either.

On July 1, 2014, six months after my grandma passed, I dreamt that my grandma, and other people I did not recognize, were on clouds. It felt like we were in heaven because the sky was light blue, and we were all standing on clouds. I was shocked that I did not know what to say or do to my grandma. Meanwhile, my grandma held her arm out for a hug, but I did not want to hug her and break her bones. I still tried to hug her, but I was so scared. The other people there told me it was okay to hug her. As soon as I hugged her, I woke up, and all I did was cry because I missed her so much. To me, the dream symbolized that everything would be alright in life, but I could not tell.

* * *

Here's some advice:

How would you react to finding out news about a family member's betrayal right after burying a loved one? Being angry, overwhelmed, and hurt are normal! Try not to take it personally; their choices shouldn't affect how you react. Life is out of your control, and it can be scary, but learn how to be positive and spin the situation.

Dreams about your loved ones are so complex. You dream about them, but then when you wake up, they're not there, and it seems so evil, but comforting. So always appreciate the dreams about your loved ones because it means more than what actually occurred.

REALITY SET IN

On September 1, 2014, it was the first Labor Day without my grandma, and it was the worst. It was the last time I went to the Arkabutla Dam. I tried to look for my grandma, but I forgot she was dead. I did not care about going to the Arkabutla Dam after my grandma died. I was with Destiny and Raven, and we talked about school and how their families were doing. I had spaghetti, corn, ribs, and beans. Everything tasted good until I got to the spaghetti. At first, when I ate the spaghetti, it was not as bad, but then there was an odd aftertaste. I asked Destiny and Raven, "Who made this spaghetti?" Raven replied, "It was Aunt Shannon."

It was then that I realized why my grandmother never wanted anything that she cooked. We all laughed while we spat the nastiness from our mouths onto the ground. We finally were done eating and went back to play on the playground and the swings until it was time to go home.

On the ride back home, I knew it was going to be the last time I went to that place. The energy was weird, and all I could think about was how much better it was with my grandma.

Christmas 2014 was the saddest Christmas ever, but all the grand-kids tried being in the Christmas spirit. When I tell you nobody had

Christmas spirit, I mean nobody did. We ate food my granddad and his girlfriend had prepared. Yes, they were still together, which killed my whole vibe knowing she was there. She was not my grandma, not even a step-grandma.

In the past, when my grandma was alive, there were many presents, but this year, there were no presents under the tree, nor did anyone bring a gift. No presents were passed out that year. Typically, my grandparents would give us all $50 on a card, but that did not happen. My granddad was not my grandma. My grandma would have had gifts for everyone and vice versa.

My cousin Destiny passed out letters to all her cousins. Mine read:

Hi Ashley. The first thing that pops into my head when I think about you is your smile because whenever I see you, you are always smiling. You are so short! But I love you unconditionally. Even though I do not see you and Imani as much as I like, when I do, it is some of the best times we have ever shared. The fact that we lost grandma so soon shows me that you should always love your family and never take them for granted. She took a substantial chunk out of everyone's heart when she left. It was so hard on us, even though you never showed it. She was the "Super Glue" that held the entire Davis Family together. Now that she is gone, we all are slowly shifting apart. I hope this Christmas will bring us all back together. I love you, Ashley.

One thing about me is that I would smile through any and everything. Therefore, Destiny thought I never showed my hurt. On the inside, I was weak mentally and emotionally drained. The truth was, I cried nonstop behind closed doors because all I could do was cry. I could not call my grandma anymore. I was lost because I spent so much time with my grandma, and now that she was gone, I did not know how I was supposed to live when my life revolved around her. How could I pick my life up and act like her death did not change anything?

That Christmas explained how much of an impact my grandma had on the family. The note had me in tears because it felt like my family had fallen apart, but that note also gave me hope.

Everyone stayed until midnight; afterward, everybody went home.

Before my sister left for college in January 2015, we went to my granddad's house twice to spend time with him since my grandma was no longer alive. The first time we went, it was silent most of the time because my granddad did not talk much. My sister asked most of the questions because she knew how to start a conversation. My granddaddy has always been the quiet type who gives short answers.

After about an hour of me mostly saying yes and Imani trying to make conversation, we left. On the car ride back, my sister told me my granddad never secured or paid for my grandma's headstone for her grave. I looked at my sister and asked, "What do you mean he did not pay for a headstone? He had all his retirement money, but what about the insurance money?"

She cried and said that she did not know. I thought about how I was just saying to myself I love him, but now I love him a little less. I thought, "How could you not give my grandma a headstone? You cried at her burial like you cared. So, what happened to that man?"

The next time we visited, I tried not to think about the fact that he didn't give my grandma a headstone. I still greeted him with love, as always, and like the last visit, we barely talked much. You could say my sister did most of the talking. My sister talked about her life, and she went down memory lane and talked about grandma, and how fun it used to be as kids. We finally left because it was getting dark, and Mississippi dark means pitch-black.

As we drove back home, my sister turned to me and said she had been asking my granddad for grandma's jewelry, and he still would not give my sister my grandma's necklaces that she wanted so badly. I told her she had to stop trying to get it because he acted like he couldn't give out my grandma's necklace, but also didn't want to put money down on a headstone! *Now how does that work?* It broke my heart to say that to my big sister, but it had to be said because she had been asking for a year without an answer. I just didn't understand how he couldn't give my sister the necklace. My grandma actually wouldn't mind. We thought he had all my grandma's jewelry, but we were unsure. I thought, "Why did we even go over there?" I was so happy to see him, but then when we left, the real him started to appear, and I started to get disappointed in my granddad. *How did he manage to make me so happy to see him? Then, when I'm not there, his actions break my heart?*

* * *

Here's some advice:

Holidays will never be the same without the glue in the family. Reality sets in, and you realize that person was the glue. So, then what now? Trying to maintain traditions can help, but there will always be a feeling that the events aren't the same. Holidays are tough without your loved ones, and it's okay to be sad or happy, but remember to make the holidays the best you can. Family can either lift your spirit, crush your spirit, or both. Knowing your loved one isn't who they really are can hurt, but remember God's got them.

DOWNHILL SPIRAL

On April 18, 2015, my granddad got married to Claudia. I did not attend because I could not be in church with hate in my spirit. I could not believe that after a year, my granddad was remarrying. That fat-necked head bastard married this fat bald head lady, calling it marriage. She was marrying a leftover man. He was already married with kids and grandchildren. She didn't win anything, but an old wrinkled man who was good for nothing.

My dad and Aunt Candice attended the wedding— God bless their souls. They went because my granddad begged my dad to be his best man. My Aunt Candice went because she loved her father and wanted to support him. Of course, my dad loved his dad as well, so he agreed.

On that day, I decided instead to take the ACT and went out with my then-boyfriend to take my mind off the fact that my granddad had married somebody else so soon, and to top it off, it was the negative-spirited lady who visited my grandma in the hospital.

After they were married, he gave her a big wedding ring and a brand-new car. Everybody began to ask where Grandma's jewelry was that he still hadn't given anyone. The whole family thought he pawned all her jewelry and sold her clothes. We thought it would be a good thing to give the grandchildren a piece of her legacy. My heart broke so bad on this day because he married someone else so suddenly when he just cried over my grandma a year and a half ago. *Were his tears real?* Anger was burning through my heart because yet again, he was such a disappointment of a granddad.

One day over the summer, my granddad asked all his grandchildren to come to his house because he wanted a family reunion with his side of the family and my grandma's side of the family, which was why I wanted to go. I enjoyed being around my family, and family mattered more since my grandma died. So, I decided to go.

My sister drove us to my granddad's house, and when we arrived, my cousins Destiny and Gabrielle stood waiting for some of the grandchildren to come. There was a beige tent set up where the table and food were, so we went to the tent to get some food. As I fixed my plate, a lady pinched my butt. I was so shocked, that I turned around and tried not to swing. The lady said, "Aww, my bad, baby. I thought you were somebody else."

I found it weird that a grown person would do that. I let that go and began looking for somewhere to sit, but there was no one sitting. My sister and I stood by a blue Cadillac car and ate on the car's hood. As we ate, we were joined by my other cousins, Clyde and Millie, who were on my granddad's side, and were around my sister's age. We talked about who we had seen so far and whom we knew. Then, I asked who those people were because I did not recognize anyone. Everybody said they had no idea, which meant, as you could guess, it was Claudia's family.

Everybody was angry and filled with rage because we were lied to about the situation. We could not stay mad for too long because we were around each other, but I texted my then-boyfriend and told him I hoped my granddad and his wife would burn in hell. I never talked that way about anybody, but at that moment, I was shocked and heartbroken that he had to lie. All I did was try to love him, but he was such a disappointment of a man, and this was it. I honestly said his "now wife" could be burned more in hell than him because I believed my granddad could not be like this, and he just did not know how to manage the loss of my grandma.

My cousins Markail, Destiny, and Raven joined us, and Markail said my granddad's wife's daughter had a mustache, but he would still hit that. Everybody looked at him like he was sick, calling her a man and saying he would still hit it. We all took turns asking him why though. He said, "She was fine, so I would overlook her mustache."

We all busted out laughing and changed the subject. My sister then suggested we should all visit Grandma's grave. We all agreed, and we ditched the gathering or whatever type of party was happening and went to the grave because the grave site was only five minutes away.

We left and began to walk through the graves, looking at people's headstones to find my grandma's grave. We saw the first name of my granddad's wife Claudia on a headstone, and Raven said, "Wrong one." We laughed because we all thought my granddad's wife should have been in the ground.

We turned around, and there was grandma's grave with no head-stone, like my sister said, with a little fence around her name. I thought my grandma deserved more than this little fence. We got somebody to take a picture of us by grandma's grave so we could never forget that day. I could not believe my granddad would not take care of my grandma's headstone, which really showed how much he really did not care about her. The hurt and anger became so intense that I was beginning to hate him. It was so crazy that I realized I hated one of the only people I wanted to run to and hug. I hated how he destroyed our beautiful family relationship with his manipulative ways.

I hate him... I hate him... I hate him. Why does he keep breaking my heart and getting my hopes up and getting away with this? It's so unfair. I'm heartbroken trying to stay strong and forgive, but no more.

I didn't forgive him this time; this was too far. I really thought he changed, but he had shown that he would never change.

He says he loves his family, but how could it be love? Is it love? If so, then I don't want this.

On Thanksgiving 2015, we all went to my Aunt Candice's house. I thought my granddad and his new wife would show up, but at this point, he knew that we did not want to see her and barely wanted to see him. I just wanted to see Granddad again for the holidays like how it used to be. Sounds dumb, but I still wanted him around no matter what he did.

I went to my Aunt's house with my sister. My mom went by herself because she stayed longer and talked, and my dad drove by himself because he was always ready to go back home. We arrived at my Aunt's house and went in and hugged everyone and said hey, and surprisingly, we weren't the last ones to arrive. The last people were cousins Gabrielle and Raven. When they arrived, it was time to eat. We all stood in the kitchen and prayed over the food and how thankful we were for each other. The grandchildren fixed our food first. We had ham, greens, turkey, spaghetti, dressing, cornbread, rolls, macaroni and cheese, yams, and chitlins. I grabbed everything except chitlins because I couldn't get past the smell. I was so disappointed with the dressing because it had bones in it. My grandma would never put bones in dressing. Shame on my auntie. The rest of the food was great, and I sat with my cousins in the dining room. That marked our spot where we could talk "freely" without our parents. I say "freely" because they were one room over; however, we couldn't talk that loudly about some topics.

After we all ate, we just sat with our bellies full and continued to talk until everybody was ready to leave. After about an hour after we ate, we all decided it was time to leave, hoping to see everyone that Christmas.

* * *

Here's some advice:

Being a Christian isn't always easy. In Christianity, you are supposed to always forgive, and it is easier said than done. But what about if the disrespect is over and over? To let someone get you to the point of hate is never a good idea. In the Bible, it says to not hate. It's okay to be upset, cry, and feel heartbroken because you should always let your feelings out. Still, trust in the Lord during the process. Family is everything in dark times, and talking to family can help you get through a lot.

MINOR MED

I n March 2016, my dad drove me home from school. I had just eaten, and I remember him telling me he needed my help to get him to the Minor Med. I agreed, and we got in the car, and I was his guide to the Minor Med. I asked my dad why we needed to go to the Minor Med, and he said, "Your step-grandfather has passed away." I wondered how that happened. My dad explained that my step-grandfather was mowing the lawn with his four-wheeler, and it flipped over. For the life of me, I could not figure out exactly how it happened.

The rest of the car ride was silent except when I gave him directions to the Minor Med. We arrived, parked across the street, and proceeded to walk across the road to the Minor Med. We went up this ramp to figure out where my step-granddad was, and upon walking the halls, we first saw my uncle. My Uncle Willie struggled to stand up because he had bad knees. He told us which room and followed us in. The doctor was on his computer typing in all the information since my step-granddad had just died.

There by the bedside was Granddad and his wife, and beside me was my Uncle Willie's wife Shaquana. My Aunt Shaquana asked about the envelope by his feet, but everybody ignored her question. Then, my granddad's wife asked why my step great-granddad was still bleeding. Mind you, I was about to pass out because I did not like looking at dead people with or without a white cover on them. I wondered why she cared so much about my step-granddad when she was just my grandfather's wife. So my Aunt asked again about the envelope, and my granddad's wife said it should go to her because she he was his niece.

I thought about what she said. The conversation continued with my grandfather's wife Claudia coming to the foot of my step-grandfather's bed, and she and my Aunt started arguing about the envelope. They argued about who should get the envelope. This was such a ghetto move for me. This man had just died, and they stood there arguing by a cold foot. The argument got so heated that we all had to step out of the room as my Aunt stated how my granddad's wife was ruining the family.

In my head, I was saying, "Yes, Auntie. Tell her like it is." My grandfather's wife continued to say that my Aunt was unfaithful to Uncle Willie. I thought, "Well, to be fair, my uncle had a child while dating my Aunt by somebody else, but that was not my place to intervene." The argument shut down when my granddad called my Aunt a winch. I had not heard anybody say that since 2007–2008. At this point, it was time to go because my granddad wanted to act like a tough guy and tried to protect his rusty, crusty, dusty wife. After that, everybody went home.

When we got home, I went upstairs to cry and ask God why my family was so messed up. I asked grandma why she had to leave me with those people. My conscience told me to get up because that situation had nothing to do with me. I was just upset that it happened and that she was gone. Here we go again, thinking of Granddad so highly, and he disappointed me again.

* * *

Here's some advice:

Shock, confusion, and anger are normal when you don't understand why adults act the way they do. Sometimes you think your family could really come together, but it is so much of a deeper level for everyone feeling toward grief and betrayal. To hear people argue about nonsense can be overwhelming, but remember, it has nothing to do with their emotions. Just always pray about things.

CELEBRATION

May 2016 was my graduation from high school. I was so excited to ditch high school and enter the world of college. My graduation day was insane. I ran around the night before and the morning of to get ready. My cousin Kenneth spent the night so that he could make it to my graduation, which was filled with nothing but craziness. We went from hitting each other with pillows that night to him helping me paint my toenails for my big day.

The morning arrived, and it was a different kind of crazy. Of course, we rushed because my sister took forever to do my makeup because she woke up late. My sister was doing my makeup and curling my hair so I could look my best. She was better at that stuff than I was. After about an hour, she was finished with me and had to do her own makeup and hair, which took another two hours. After that, everybody was dressed and ready. I was excited because Markail and I were graduating on the same day. It was not only on the same day, but his ceremony was right after mine in the same building.

My sister drove Kenneth and me, and my mom rode with my dad. Of course, hanging out with my sister and Kenneth was always a blast. We turned the music up and laughed the whole way there. I wished my grandma would have been alive to see me graduate. That would have completed my day. We finally made it, and I could not put my graduation hat on. I could not figure out why, so I asked my sister if she could put it on for me. She did so with honor. Kenneth took a photo of the special moment.

I entered the building downtown so I could line up for graduation. When I walked out to the graduation ceremony, I was nervous because all eyes were on me, and I did not like attention, but I did it for the graduation. I was honestly ready for the graduation party and to see all my family. It was finally my turn to walk across after thirty minutes of speeches. I was more than ready. I was so ready that I slick-tripped when I walked up the stairs toward the stage (nobody saw that). I walked across proudly and was ready to go home.

After graduation, the class received their diplomas, so I proceeded to find my family. It was a great feeling to see my family come to support me. My mom, dad, sister Imani, cousins Kenneth and Leana, mom's brother and his girlfriend, and Aunt Pamela all supported me, which was amazing.

After tons of photos, my sister drove Kenneth, Leana, and me home together; we all hung out together because of how close in age we were. As we went back to my house, we jammed to music and screamed, "Wooooooh!" to publicize my big day.

My sister also graduated that month, so we decided to have a combined graduation party at the house since we invited the same family members, but different friends. As we drove home, Imani and I began setting up last-minute decorations for the party, and then the party started. My mom's side of the family came. They always came through. The four grandchildren on my dad's side came. Markail came, and I gave him my congratulations, and we took many selfies. All the grandchildren who came over took a group photo, which meant so much because no matter what happened, we were all still going to be there for each other.

I was so overwhelmed with different emotions because seeing them made up for my grandma not being there. In my heart, I still wanted her there so I could make her proud. Overall, the party turned out great.

After not seeing my granddad, I started to instead focus on grief. I focused on grief by understanding I was still in the sadness stage because I was achieving life, and my grandma wasn't there to see it in person. Instead, I turned to my family for support. They won't replace grandma, but in a way, their presence makes up for her loss. Moments like taking pictures with family are always priceless and are some of the best memories.

* * *

Here's some advice:

Taking time to enjoy family and accomplishments is needed. To have support really does help with happiness. We take celebrations for granted, which we shouldn't, because life is too short not to enjoy. Milestones without your loved ones hurt, and it's okay to be a little sad because they're not there, but focusing on who does show up counts, as well.

THE START OF FORGIVENESS

T hat fall, I attended Austin Peay State University. Freshman year was good; I had no issues. However, my sophomore year of college was the worst year of college for me. I took eighteen credit hours, worked part-time at Subway, and modeled. I went to four classes on MWF and two on TTh. Afterward, I went straight to work and had homework right after that. I worked from 2:00 p.m.–8:00 p.m., and on the days I modeled, I was off from Subway, which gave me more time to finish my homework.

I was so stressed that I became addicted to Coca-Cola and ate cookies from Subway to cope with everything. In college, you find unusual ways to cope with life, and I chose drinking Coke. My mindset was so gone from trying to deal with the grief from my grandma's death, thoughts about everything my granddad did over the years, the schoolwork became too much, and work was work, so all that combined made me completely numb. I did not care anymore about school or my social life. I was so burned out that I did not know what to do. It got so bad that I drank Coke out of a bottle like it was water. I ate three to four cookies every shift, which was five times a week. I turned to ice cream or a milkshake if Coca-Cola was not available. I cried so much that year that I had multiple mental breakdowns because I could not handle all of it at once. Strong people break, and I broke completely in half and still never understood how I made it through that year. The only reason I went so hard in school was that I wanted to get my associate degree and not fall behind. I realized it was my mistake to take on so much.

In April 2018, my cousin sent all of us an invite to her prom. I was excited to go but knew I would see Granddad. I had not seen him since the Minor Med incident, and the thought of seeing him made me hyperventilate and cry so hard. I hated that every time I thought about seeing him up until that point, I would be shaking and crying because I was hurting so much. I felt that when I saw him again, something else would come about, which was never good, but I agreed to go. I wanted to truly forgive him.

Every day before the prom, I prepared myself. I tried to let my walls down by talking through every situation out loud so that I could take back control over my emotions. I thought if I talked a lot aloud to myself, I could help myself. I thought "How could such a person whom I always thought was kind and nice turn out to be the biggest liar and narcissistic person who broke my heart even more after my grandma died?" I had enough of crying till my eyes were red and puffy.

On April 30, 2018, my cousin Raven's prom day arrived. My sister said she would go, and I was home from college that weekend, so it sounded like the perfect plan. We lived in Arlington, Tennessee, which was far from Mississippi. It was a two-hour drive, which was too long for me. I was thankful my sister Imani volunteered to drive. The whole ride was filled with music, and we talked most of the way, which helped take my mind off the fact that I had to see Granddad. We talked about how funny it would be to see Raven in a dress because my grandma always made fun of how Raven looked. My grandma always said that Raven was built like a man.

When we arrived, we knew it was some real Mississippi country stuff. Her prom send-off was in the center of a shopping center. I asked my sister about where we were supposed to park because it was not clear. My sister ended up parking in a good parking spot right in the middle. My cousin Raven came out from a black truck in a mainly blue dress with silver sparkles and a silver band along the hem of her dress. Of course, my sister and I took pictures and helped Raven fix her hair and dress when needed. Then, right before my eyes stood my granddad as he smiled and laughed like he was not the evil man who created so much drama, but I remembered my purpose was to forgive and heal.

My sister and I walked over to him. I whispered to myself, "Okay, here we go." We both said, "Hey, Granddad."

He replied, "Heeeey," with his arms wide open like he was not the same person who spewed out lies, saying that we did not love him. He must have thought that we did not know or that all should be forgiven. Again, I reminded myself I was there to forgive and let go of the hate, so we hugged him. That hug made me want to cry because all I ever wanted from him was a hug. I wanted somebody to run to for comfort, but instead, all I got was hurt, lies, betrayal, and rejection. None of it mattered when we hugged though, which was a great sign. The hug reminded me of when my grandma first died, and I needed a comforting hug.

I wish I could say that the hug healed everything, but unfortunately, that was only the first step of forgiveness and healing. After we hugged, we took a picture. It was a picture I would never see again, of course, because he never gave anything back. I had to remind myself again that things were in the past, and right now, I was there to start the process of forgiveness.

We went back to take more photos of Raven before the sun went down, and then she went to her prom. Her prom was memorable. We were ecstatic at the thought that Raven was the last grandbaby to have a prom. So, when she invited us, it was an easy decision to go. Raven finally got into a black limo to go to prom, and everybody started to leave. So we left, as well.

Since that hug in April, I called my granddad once a week. I tried to establish a bond with him. I set up a day to visit him, which was June 15. I thought it would be a fantastic time to bond with my grandfather because June 15 was his birthday and Father's Day, too.

Before I visited Granddad's house, I visited my Uncle Willie's house, who lived across the road from my granddad. I had not been to his house in a while and wanted to check in on him.

I parked in my Uncle Willie's driveway. Upon my arrival, I saw that they had puppies on the front porch. I am not afraid of puppies, but I would not go near puppies until the owner said it was fine. I got out of my car, and I walked up to their stairs carefully. I did so because it felt like the stairs were not able to support me walking across them, which should have been a red flag to turn around, but I proceeded up anyway. Somebody slick broke their stairs, and I almost fell through. As I walked across the porch, I saw the puppies more closely and thought they were cute. Next thing you know, a huge German shepherd on a chain came from underneath the porch. The dog ran up the stairs and was a few inches from me. I stopped breathing and pounded on my uncle's door. I hoped that he would answer before I peed on myself or got chewed up by this dog. I saw my life flash before my eyes, and I started praying to God.

My uncle finally opened the door and said, "Hey, I guess the girl dog liked you." He laughed. I replied, "Umm, I almost died out there" with the straightest face ever. "You know, I stopped breathing just to save my life." That made him laugh even more, like my life was a joke.

I came in just to see how he was and how he felt about how his children's lives were going. We talked about how his son Hakeem went down the wrong path in life, and my uncle told me it was his parenting that led his son down the wrong path. I thought to myself, "You're supposed to set an example for your children."

I asked how he felt about his daughter Gabrielle getting engaged so quickly. He stared at me because she had only known him for about five to six months. By seeing his expression, I could tell that he was not too pleased. I usually made jokes about my grandma coping with everything, but my uncle was not in the joking process of grief at all.

I often made jokes about how she would drop me off at before-care in elementary school and would get mad because the before-care workers were not there because we always arrived there before them.

My uncle started to cry and said, "Well, at least she kept you. She never kept my kids." I thought, "Well, this conversation just went left."

My Uncle Willie said that since he was a "troubled" young adult, he went to jail a lot. I stopped listening and thought about what this had to do with my grandma keeping us sometimes. Then, I thought to myself about him being a troubled youth— that was funny! I reminded myself to be sympathetic because he cried in front of me, but having sympathy in that moment for him did not work. I stared at him, and instantly, I changed the subject. I told him that I was there to see his dad.

He said, "Awww, yes, he should be home." I hoped that was the case since I called him before I drove two hours for a visit.

I got up to hug my uncle and tell him that I loved him. I also told him before I came over next time that I would call him. He laughed and agreed, and I walked to my granddad's house across the road. I went around the front door to knock, but no one answered, so I went to the back door, and there he was. He opened the back door, and we greeted each other with a hug and a hey. I wanted a house tour because I had not been there in years. I was excited to start this bond with my granddad.

When I walked around, I noticed that there were no pictures of my grandma anywhere. I thought about where my grandma's photo was. I expected this was because he had moved on, but I had not moved on from seeing her pictures. I returned to the kitchen, and his wife cooked. On my journey to forgiveness, I decided to give her a chance and thought everything was a miscommunication. I just wanted to hope that these were not the people who were this nasty and spiteful toward the family, but they were. I gave them a chance to do better and gave myself a chance to regain control of my emotions.

We barely talked; his wife told me how she and my granddad were high school sweethearts. I then understood why they got together so quickly because they had already been with each other before.

I drove home and tried to convince myself that this method of forgiveness would help me.

Thanksgiving 2018 was one of the funniest, ever. That year,

Thanksgiving was hosted by my Aunt Candice. It had been the second or third time she had hosted since my grandma was gone. It had been the most peaceful family gathering, despite everything that happened. It was a picture-perfect, most comfortable socialization family gathering we had. I was back in town from college and was ecstatic to see my family and eat delicious food. Of course, I rode with my sister because my dad always left too soon, and my mom always stayed too late, which I was not planning on either. I did not want to drive my car, so I ended up in my sister's car. My sister has always been late to events, and I do not mean thirty minutes. I mean, she arrives one and a half or two hours late for every function. My Aunt Candice's house was down the street from my sister's home, so she took her time to get there.

I did not mind because I never go on time, but I was never as late as my sister. My cousin Markail blew my phone up to see where we were. I told him we were on the way and would not want to miss Thanksgiving dinner because we missed everybody. We finally arrived, and as we walked through the door, my Uncle Willie was sitting by the food table because of his bad knees. We both went up to him to say hey and hug him. The whole family was at my Aunt's house —Uncle Willie, Aunt Shaquana, Aunt Candice, my mom, my dad, Destiny, Raven, Gabrielle, Hakeem, and Markail—and everything turned out great because all of us were together.

The food was ready and prepared, so we stood in a circle to pray over the delicious food. Everybody made their plates. The grandchildren made their plates first, as the adults were right behind us. The grandbabies were in the dining room, and the adults were in the living room. We had fun in the dining room. We talked about how life was and how good the food was until I ate the dressing. I love dressing, but once again, my Aunt Candice put bones in the dressing. She did that every year. And every year, my entire Thanksgiving was ruined. Gabrielle said she made her dressing, but I never saw it. We also had ham, greens, rolls, spaghetti, yams, mac and cheese, and chitterlings.

This Thanksgiving was so different for so many reasons. First, we were older, and a lot of the grandchildren smoked weed. So, after we ate, my cousins Markail, Destiny, and Hakeem wanted to go smoke. And for no reason at all, Raven saw her brother wanted to partake. She yelled out to their dad, Uncle Willie, as soon as Markail, Destiny, and Hakeem were about to leave to smoke. She tried to snitch, and Hakeem looked at Raven like, "Really? We are too old to snitch!" Everybody else died of laughter because of how embarrassed Hakeem was. It was 30 minutes until we stopped laughing, and Markail and Destiny left without Hakeem.

We continued to talk, and Hakeem kept staring at Raven. She kept asking Hakeem, "What?" Hakeem asked why she would do that. She laughed and got on her phone. We were all so full, and of course, we took home leftovers.

The time I spent with my family always made me happy— not sure if it was the family support or just something to look forward to with my family. Those were the moments I cherished most, especially how we would roast each other and just have fun together.

* * *

Here's some advice:

The thing to remember is to give yourself grace. When starting out, if you're still angry, it is okay. I was still so angry and hurt, but remember, forgiveness is for you. I always thought the concept of forgiveness was that it should be done as soon as possible, but it is okay to slowly forgive. I started with a hug and a talk, then I visited my granddad. Take it slow, and remember, it is to take control of your emotions. Don't allow anyone to control your emotions.

NEW BEGINNING

For the remainder of my spring semester, I debated whether I should go to the U of M or not. My mom told me that the room and board were too much and that I could only stay at Austin Peay if I got a scholarship. I applied for a scholarship that I thought would help when I had a recommendation from one of my teachers, and I still did not receive the scholarship; no other scholarship I applied for contacted me either. I slick did not want them to contact me. I was so over my life at Austin Peay. I thought about what kept me at Austin Peay and decided why not go home? I made a pros and cons list to help.

My first pro to staying at Austin Peay was freedom, which was huge for me because I loved to be independent. My other pro was that I saved money at Austin Peay because I walked to class, which saved on gas. My next pro was my only friend there. That was it. My cons were roommates. I disliked every roommate I ever had in college. My next con was that I was unhappy. I only worked and went to class, which was my fault, but I had to stay focused on school. Another con was that I was homesick and hated to drive back to Memphis when I could already be there with my family.

My first pro to attending the University of Memphis was being closer to my family, which excited me because I missed being able to hang out with them on the weekends. Another reason was for a fresh start. I could meet new people who could connect me with Memphis Law School. My last pro was that I had no roommate; I had the whole upstairs to myself. My con was I had to give up my freedom, which was the biggest thing, but it would only be temporary (a couple of years). My next con was finding a job back home, which was sometimes hard when I came home, and I did not want to work in fast food, so that process would take a while.

After making my list, I decided it was in my best interest to transfer to the University of Memphis. I decided it would be best for my mental health as well. At Austin Peay, life was sucked out of me, and I was tired of being there, floating daily. So I submitted my application in March, and a month later, in April, I was accepted. I immediately put in my two weeks' notice at work since I found out the news at work. As soon as I clocked out, I called my mom, and we both were so overjoyed. She was happier than me because her baby would be home. It was not easy, but I wanted to be more comfortable in a better space with better food.

When I finally went to my dorm after work, I called my sister to tell her what I decided, which was to come home. To my surprise, my sister and I got into an intense argument, which was the most painful argument we had ever had. I started by telling her the news, and she told me she knew it, and I asked what she meant. She told me, "Yeah, ever since you failed that class, of course, Mom wanted you to come home." I explained, "Just because I failed one class did not mean I had to come home."

My sister said she was convinced that was the real reason I was coming back. Then, I asked her how that was. When every semester my mom asked me to come home, even during the semesters, I did my best. I did my absolute best at Austin Peay until sophomore year, and my mom asked me to go to the University of Memphis, since I was at Central. At Central, I was in honors and maintained over a 3.5 GPA. So, how?

She kept bringing up the fact that I had failed a class the semester before. The class broke me badly mentally because of the amount of work I had to do, and I just stopped trying. I did not want to be reminded of that because I did great my next semester. After both of us tried to explain our reasoning, I ended the argument, and we changed the conversation. Then, I had homework to do and said I would call her the following day. Honestly, after that call, I broke down crying because being reminded of how stressful that class had made me was depressing, but also motivated me to do better. I still held on to my reasons why I wanted to go to the University of Memphis.

I packed my dorm up, quit my job with joy, and went back home weeks later after I passed my exams. I headed home to start a new journey and hoped I could find a job and go back to school, but not be as stressed.

$$* * *$$

Here's some advice:

Some people develop addictions while trying to get through challenging situations. There will be seasons of life that are harder than others and may cause intense stress. Try reaching out for more help. Consider finding new hobbies or having self-care time to minimize the stress.

A BRAND "NEW START"

I went back home to Memphis to start my stress-free summer. I had a summer job, and I finally dyed my hair red. First, it started as streaks to see if I really wanted my whole head red.

Moving back home and dyeing my hair was a step into my new beginning. The next thing I wanted to do was spend more time with my family. I wanted to also get my mind together for school and for myself.

But my new start was nothing like what I expected…

Acknowledgments

I am immensely grateful to my immediate family for their unwavering support and boundless love during the most challenging moments of this journey. To my mom, thank you for being there for me, driving me to see my grandma, and providing solace and understanding during my moments of grief. To my dad, you were the first to take me to visit my grandma and allowed me cherished moments at her home. Your support meant the world to me. To my sister, thank you for standing by my side, ensuring I didn't face grief and forgiveness alone, and driving me to visit our grandma.

To the entire Davis family, thank you for your support and for coming together to make the best out of the challenging circumstances surrounding grandma's passing. A heartfelt appreciation goes to Aunt Carmen and my cousin Aaronis for their presence at the funeral, offering comfort and a sense of togetherness during that difficult time.

To my granddad, you have been a profound source of inspiration for this book.

My gratitude extends to my late grandma, who served as the glue holding our family together. Your strength and resilience continue to resonate within me, shaping the person I am today. Your role in shaping my perspective cannot be overstated. Thank you for being the driving force behind my words. I carry your spirit with me, always.

Thank you, Vision Publishing House, for your support throughout this journey.

Lastly, I would like to express my sincere appreciation to everyone who played a part in supporting me throughout this transformative journey. Your encouragement, guidance, and unwavering belief in me have been invaluable.

A special shout-out goes to my early supporters:

Aaronis Turner
Angela Gatewood
Wanda Davis
Jordan Davis
Jasmine Thomas
Jasmine Williams
Carmen Turner
Angela Buchanan
Bria Harris
Dior Robinson
Rhonda Davis
Ryan Thomas
Jasmine Holt
Tricia Cruciotti
Austin Oliver III

Thank you all for supporting this special project
that is near and dear to my heart!

ABOUT THE AUTHOR

Ashley Davis, a native of Memphis, TN, is a talented African American author and legal investigator. With a deep passion for writing, Ashley has transformed her love for storytelling into the creation of her debut book.

Born and raised in a close-knit family, Ashley's strong sense of kinship has greatly influenced her life and writing journey. It is this profound connection to family that fuels her heartfelt commitment to her craft, making this book a deeply personal and significant endeavor.

Drawing upon her unique background and experiences, Ashley brings a fresh perspective to her storytelling, infusing her narratives with authenticity, humor, and relatability. As an author, she aims to captivate readers, leaving an indelible impression that resonates long after the last page is turned.

Stay connected with Ashley Davis as she continues to inspire and captivate audiences with her powerful storytelling. Follow her on social media and join her on this remarkable literary journey.

facebook.com/ashley.davis.5055
instagram.com/bona_fide_ashley
tiktok.com/@adavis1230

www.ingramcontent.com/pod-product-compliance
Lightning Source LLC
Chambersburg PA
CBHW051544120626
46551CB00013B/1358